Vocational Vision:

Defining Your Talent for a Successful Career

Valerie Schmidt

USA

ISBN 978-0-557-23152-2
LCCN

Printed in the United States of America.

Preface

This book is dedicated to all employees, managers, executives, and business owners who are ready to do the work they love and be paid for it. I hope you will use this book as a guide to creating a personal job description, roles, and responsibilities that satisfy and fulfill you personally, professionally, and financially. The steps provided in this book work for everyone; regardless of whether you're at the beginning, middle, transitioning, or retirement phase and whether you are technical, creative, logical, practical, or all (or none) of the above. Vocational Vision will provide you with the insight and steps you need to have a career that you will look forward to each day. Building a career around what we love is unfortunately often a dream that we deny ourselves. There is a myth that work must be dull, monotonous, or personally unfulfilling in order for someone to pay you to do it. Guess what? You can do work that you love to do and still receive good financial compensation. Are you surprised? Are you willing to believe it? I challenge you to give *Vocational Vision: Defining Your Talent for a Successful Career* a try. I am convinced the program will work for you.

Sadly, having a satisfying career isn't something that most of us do automatically. In my experience, there are no university courses that teach the example that our careers can be wonderful and fun. And, let's be honest; it may be simple but it also takes desire, commitment, and action. Just like learning how to use a new defense system, we have to understand the underlying design before we can accurately apply it.

The Vocational Vision program works. I know this from the experiences of my clients and because I use it too. It will work for you too! It will change the way you look at opportunities and tasks that come your way. You will know what elements need to be in place for you to experience satisfaction and the inner knowledge that comes from doing the work you were meant to do. You will have a customized plan that you can use to create, nurture, and build your perfect career.

I promise you this; using the Vocational Vision program will definitely raise your awareness about what you truly want. Give yourself the gift of working the plan and using it to discover the vision that defines the talents and skills you were meant to use in your work! You can be successful, happy, and personally enriched – and find enjoyment each and every day.

Acknowledgements

First, I want to thank my husband, Dave, who encouraged me in writing this book. He believed in me and held me accountable when I felt like fudging on my plan.

I also want to thank my mother, Elberta, for keeping me excited and enthusiastic about her daughter "writing a book." That excitement and the undesirable thought of possibly disappointing her brought me back to my laptop many times.

To my friend and retired English teacher, Gloria, thank you for your timely reviews. You were my safety net for writing and grammar and helped me move forward with less fear of the comma and semi-colon!

To Joan, Natalie, Jane, Bert, Vicki, and Sylvia thank you for giving me your quiet and unshakable confidence in my ability to do this work.

To my colleague and friend, Jim, thank you for pushing me to get started, for keeping me going, for reading every single page in your precious spare time and for giving me your valuable input as a published author.

There are so many other people in my life that have encouraged me, hounded me when I needed it, and whose friendship and belief in me made the journey a wonderful experience.

Thank you all very much.

Contents

Chapter One

1

What is the Vocational Vision Program?

Life and Career Changes do not need to be difficult or filled with the likelihood of failure. You can minimize your risk in any life change if you approach it using the same techniques used successfully in Project Management. In *Vocational Vision: Defining Your Talent for a Successful Career*, we provide you with a Personal Project Plan and guide you step-by-step through the implementation of your own successful change.

Why it is needed

Most people approach "change" with unrealistic or unplanned expectations. It is therefore not a surprise that they often have unplanned for and unexpected results. They often give up and return to well-known and comfortable but unfulfilling work or lives. The problem comes from looking unrealistically at a life or career change.

Here are some examples of unrealistic thinking…

1. Rose-colored glasses, "...It will be easy for me to do something different if I just want it enough…"
2. Grass is greener, "…I'd really like to do what Joe does instead of what I have to do…"
3. Yearning, "…If only I could do what I want to do but I'm stuck…"
4. Desperation, "…I don't care what it is, I just want to get out of my current situation. I hate it!"

How our process helps

The process we will introduce to you makes it simple and straightforward for you to succeed in making a career or life change. By following the Vocational Vision program you will create a roadmap and project plan for change that works specifically for you.

What We Will Be Doing (i.e. the program)

In *Vocational Vision: Defining Your Talent for a Successful Career*, we provide a set of rules for creating change in a finite number of steps. The steps are based on formal methodologies used today in project management, coaching/mentoring, and career management. These formal techniques are combined with a state-of-the-art learning strategy called "Appreciative Inquiry[1]." Together these change processes will help you to:

1. Set the scope for what you want to accomplish
2. Define your change requirements
3. Identify and manage risks to implementing your changes
4. Manage your change schedule to completion

Just as in business project management, having a well-managed project plan for making changes in your life and career will put you in the top 2% of people going through a life or career change. The other 98% fail, give-up, or partially succeed. It is a sad fact that many people going through a life or career change give up on themselves in addition to giving up on their desired change. They often lose hope that it is even possible for them to change.

Using the Vocational Vision career program will propel you into that top 2% - the Successful Life and Career Changers group! More importantly, it will allow you to achieve your ultimate goals, whatever they are!

How to survive the process

The vocational Vision career program has an additional element that will help you stay on track with your change plan. We

---

[1] The Handbook of Appreciative Inquiry, Cooperrider, Whitney and Stavros

understand that during the process of change there will be challenges, setbacks, and roadblocks to overcome. Our unique process includes techniques for identifying roadblocks and setbacks, analyzing them, and mitigating their effects on your success. In *Vocational Vision: Defining Your Talent for a Successful Career*, we show you how to survive the process of change and provide yourself with a mid-process kicker anytime you need one.

When implemented properly, you will discover that you will have to work harder to fail than you will to succeed in making desirable changes in your life and career.

Join us NOW and read on to experience the easy way to making life and career changes through the Vocational Vision program!

Delve Deeper Into What Is Happening

Growth happens all around us everyday. As humans, it is normal for our lives to change over time. These changes keep us vital and lively and can keep our lives from becoming dull and uninteresting. Change creates progress in our culture, business, career, and life. Change and growth can also cause stress for us when we do not know how to manage it successfully.

Your life and career skills have changed dramatically since you left school. Your career-related compensation and recognition are usually based on your skill and leadership growth. For example, as you acquire new skills, develop your ability to work independently, and discover and practice your leadership style, you become more valuable to your employer and your salary or billable rate increases.

Change Can Happen Unexpectedly

Sometimes we initiate change and growth. At other times, changes happen unexpectedly as when a downsizing occurs with our employer or a close personal relationship ends.

We frequently do our best to just go with the flow of change and we actually do not need any formal process to adapt to the changes around us. But sometimes there is an inner recognition that we are out of sync with something or that a bigger change is needed. This awareness of a need to change our life or career in a significant way is the starting point of a major personal transition and career or life growth.

The Process of Change

We will be looking at seven major stages of change and transition. As you read through the following stages of change, see if you recognize them in other successful transitions you have experienced in your life.

Awareness - We feel that we must make a change in our life. This is a time when we ponder and explore what it is we really want for ourselves and how it is different from our current ways.

Choice - We decide that "now" is the time for us to take action and begin to change. There is a sense of choosing to be different and to do things in different ways.

Resistance - Our old habits are much easier than changing, so we easily end up on the "slippery slope" and lose momentum or interest. Our family and friends are familiar with our old ways, and they may also play a role in our resistance. This is a normal part of the change experience. Resistance gives us a chance to reaffirm our choice or modify some aspect of it.

Commitment - Our desire to change overcomes our old comfort zone. We have a clear vision of what we want to change and a deep feeling that we are ready "now."

Creation - We actively explore new opportunities in our life and/or career. We explore, ponder, experiment and allow ourselves to use the depth of our logic and creativity in making our transformation.

Acceptance - We recognize that we have reached a plateau in our transition. We really are different now. We begin to receive internal and external rewards from making our life and/or career change. Our new way of being is now the "norm" for us and we enjoy all its benefits. We grow daily by actively applying our change to the everyday events of our lives.

Integration - The new way becomes familiar and comfortable. We enjoy this new satisfying stage. We've "juiced the orange" and now have something delicious to enjoy.

Interestingly, each major stage has sub-stages that can contain some or all of the major stages. For example, in the stage of Awareness you may find yourself having a conversation in your head that sounds something like this: "...Why am I even considering this change? Everyone says I've got a good deal here, and even though I don't like it at least I understand how it all works..." This is resistance showing up in the stage of Awareness.

Implement Change Step by Step

Each stage (step) helps you move forward. However, you may:

1. Find yourself in an "endless loop" or "get stuck" on a step.
2. Move easily through a step.
3. Find deeply meaningful learning in a step.
4. Use a step to explore new opportunities you've never thought of before.

In *Vocational Vision: Defining Your Talent for a Successful Career*, we provide you with a unique set of tools and techniques that help you transition from Awareness through Integration. It provides you the framework, process, and plan to ensure your success.

Prepare for Change

Some inexpensive tools to help you:

We recommend that you collect a few, inexpensive tools as aids for your change process.

- A small journal (or PDA if you already have one) that you carry with you
- 3 x 5 index cards or sticky notes

Also:

- Create a regular block of time for working on your project plan.
    - Set aside 15 minutes or a half-hour daily just for you.
    - Put aside distractions of all kinds (family, phones, work, TV, worries, etc.) when you work on your Personal Project Plan.
- Acknowledge yourself positively each time you participate in your project time.
- Give yourself permission to progress at your own pace, but always strive to move in the direction that will accomplish your near-term objectives.
- **Visit: www.valerieschmidt.com/worksheets to find downloadable copies of the exercises in this book.**

Notes Page:

Chapter Two

2

Personal Reality Check Process

Who Am I?

Let's set the scope for what you want to accomplish by analyzing, a bit more, who you are and what you enjoy.

What are you passionate about doing with your training, education, natural skills and talents? What activities and types of projects have always come easily for you? What do you think represents a "big enough game" for you? What have you dreamed of doing with your life and career and haven't done yet?

These questions are quite provocative and you may find yourself reluctant to consider answering them honestly. Giving yourself permission to be self-honest is vital. It is the electrical impulse that will stimulate your success in a career and also in your life. So, commit right now to do this initial exercise. It will be worth your effort!

Psychologists tell us that we each have a dominant personality type. It drives how we naturally approach leadership, decision making, team participation, and the level of detail we like. There is a need for each of our natural personality types so one type is not more valuable than another. What is important is to know that you will experience greater satisfaction and more productive accomplishments when you make career and life choices that are aligned with and complement your personality type. When you choose situations that are misaligned with your personality type, instead of satisfaction and productivity, you will likely struggle to do your work and experience some degree of dissatisfaction.

Here is a quick and fun exercise to help you begin to understand your natural and dominant approach to your work life. When you are done with the exercise, ask yourself how you feel about the results. If you are surprised at them, use the blank pages at the end of this chapter to describe why. If the results seem to fit perfectly, use those pages to describe what it means to you (good or bad) to be so well understood. You can also use the blank pages at the end of this chapter to write down any notes you would like to remember.

The exercise contains a series of questions. Read each question and answer it with a short paragraph. Then go back and pick out the words and phrases that best describe how you like to approach work, projects, and interaction with your co-workers and supervisors. Circle or highlight these words and phrases that capture the essence of your "style."

To help you get started, samples of this exercise and how to use the results are provided. Try to be completely honest when you answer these questions. Resist answering them as you think you should or as you think someone else thinks you should.

Sample Questions and Answers:

Do you like to lead? Describe your ideal leadership situation. What role do you want to play? Describe your relationship with your team. How does your role benefit the project or product you are working on?

I like making decisions about big ticket things. An example would be making a decision about which features will go into the next product release. I think this helps the team have something to begin discussing even if the end result is that we make a different choice.

The role I like to play is the visionary and persuader.

What do you value most about other leaders? How do you support leaders you value? Give an example of a time when supporting a leader worked out successfully for you and brought you satisfaction. How did your contribution help create a successful result?

I value leaders who listen to others' ideas but who are not afraid to make a decision and own the resulting success or failure.

I once worked with a team of six other managers on a performance plan. One of the managers that I didn't know well brought in some spreadsheet information and a new process. Although it was more work for me to adapt my presentation to the new style, I followed the other manager's lead. I ended up liking the result very much. I think that following this unknown (to me) leader was satisfying because I learned a valuable new tool and because by working together and collaborating we created something highly effective that everyone felt a part of.

Describe your ideal work group size and composition. Do you prefer to work alone? Do small groups work best for you? Are you happy in a very large team? What role do you like to play in a team? Give an example of a great team experience. Describe the things you really liked about it.

I prefer to work in groups most of the time. I also need time to work alone. The best sized group for me is a medium-sized group, for example, 10 – 20 people per team. I also like to be part of multiple teams.

I like to play the role of advisor, visionary, and persuader on a team although if someone else is in that role and they are being effective and authentic, then I am content to play a supporting role.

A great team experience for me was when we had a poorly defined project. The team leader chose to hold team meetings to brainstorm all the possible (and useful) features that we could think of. This team leader then went back over every idea and assigned a value based upon three criteria. When this exercise was complete, every team member had a chance to voice their ideas and each idea was treated respectfully.

How do you like to be recognized for a job well done? Do you prefer public or private recognition or both? Describe your ideal form of recognition for a job well done.

I like understated recognition rather than showy recognition. And, I like being surprised. It feels good when someone recognizes my contribution and takes action without my knowing about it.

For a job well done, my most desirable recognition would be to be called in to my boss's office and be told that my name had been submitted for an award for something related to making a customer happy or saving a sale or being part of a team that accomplished something extra ordinary.

Are decisions easy for you to make? How much information do you like to gather before making a decision? Do you like to ponder or go with your instincts? How much time do you like to take before making a decision? Take a moment and describe a decision you made that you felt good about. What made that decision a good experience for you?

Decisions are never frivolous for me but I have little or no fear in making them. I like to make purposeful decisions that align with the goals I am working towards.

The process that works best for me is to gather enough information to understand the essence of the situation needing a decision and an understanding of the long-range goals the decision will affect. The size of the decision is driven by the impact it will or can have. The greater the impact the more information I like to gather. Sometimes a very important decision needs to be made quickly. When adequate research time is not possible, I trust and rely on my experience and instincts.

How much planning and detail-oriented follow up do you enjoy doing? Are you happy planning details and then checking things off of a to-do list? Would you prefer to make up your plans 'in the moment' as you go along?

I prefer to plan the planning over executing the plan details. Some things simply defy or resist being planned and so I am always on the lookout for the need for contingency plans. Making mid-course corrections and evaluating substitutions or variances is often what it takes to successfully make a plan successful. I am not too rigid however I like a medium-level sense of order and neatness. If I want a document, I want to have it in my hands in 10 minutes or less.

Continue with these examples on how to choose Work Personality Traits.

1. **Go back through the answers and highlight or circle the key qualities.**
2. **Choose the #1, most descriptive word**
3. **Repeat this process choosing the second most descriptive, the third, and so on until there are five or six key words or phrases**

Examples of Work Personality Traits:

big ticket decision making	*helps the team have something to discuss*
leaders who listen to others' ideas #4	***learned a valuable new tool #2***
we created something highly effective	*prefer to work in groups*
need time to work alone	*part of multiple teams*
Advisor	***Visionary #1***
and collaborator #1	*every team member had a voice*
Understated recognition	*like being surprised*
accomplished something extra-ordinary	*decisions are never frivolous*

no fear in making them (decisions)	***purposeful decisions #3***
Information to understand the essence	*trust and rely on my experience and instincts*
plan the planning	*lookout for the need for contingency plans*
not too rigid	

Here is an example of how to create "I AM" statements using Work Personality Traits:

I AM a visionary leader who likes to collaborate. (#1 trait)

I AM attracted to new ideas and learning new tools. (#2 trait)

I AM a purposeful decision maker. (#3 trait)

I AM a leader who values listening to others as well as being listened to. (#4 trait)

Now that you have seen an example, try the exercise for yourself.

Take Action!

Do you like to lead? Describe your ideal leadership situation. What role do you want to play? Describe your relationship with your team. How does your role benefit the project or product you are working on?

What do you value most about other leaders? How do you support leaders you value? Give an example of a time when supporting a leader worked out successfully for you and brought you satisfaction. How did your contribution help create a successful result?

Describe your ideal work group size and composition. Do you prefer to work alone? Do small groups work best for you? Are you happy in a very large team? What role do you like to play in a team? Give an example of a great team experience. Describe the things you really liked about it.

How do you like to be recognized for a job well done? Do you prefer public or private recognition or both? Describe your ideal form of recognition for a job well done.

Are decisions easy for you to make? How much information do you like to gather before making a decision? Do you like to ponder or go with your instincts? How much time do you like to take before making a decision? Take a moment and describe a decision you made that you felt good about. What made that decision a good experience for you?

How much planning and detail-oriented follow up do you enjoy doing? Are you happy planning details and then checking things off of a to-do list? Would you prefer to make up your plans 'in the moment' as you go along?

Take Action!

1. **Now, go back through your answers and highlight or circle the key qualities that seem to be really YOU.**

2. **Once you have a list of twenty or more key descriptive words and phrases, choose the ONE word or phrase that most describes you in your ideal work situation.**

3. **Repeat this process and choose the next most descriptive word or phrase until you have the top five or six key words or phases.**

4. **Use them to create your "I AM" sentence below.**

Review the examples on page 26 again, if needed, to help you get started.

Work Personality Traits:

Create your "I AM" statements.

Transfer these to your Personal Project Plan on page 137 in the section labeled "I AM Statements".

I AM ____

I AM ____

I AM ____

I AM ____

Chapter Two

Extra Worksheet Pages:

Chapter Two

Extra Worksheet Pages:

Chapter Three

3

What Do I Want?

Hopefully, you enjoyed the personality inventory exercise and your "I AM" statements either showed you something new about yourself or gave you confirmation for what you already know.

To build a strong set of requirements for your change plan, we need to drill down on what past experiences have taught you about what you like or dislike. Having this level of detail will help you set the scope for your next career move or advancement in the business world. It will also help you if your desired change is a life change outside of your current work area.

These next exercises are designed to uncover the core needs and requirements you have for an enjoyable career. You already know a lot about these from your past experiences and what you found you liked or disliked. Take a few moments and focus on what experiences from your past you would like more of.

Take Action!

Use the following workbook pages to write your answers to these questions.

(Note: If you need more space, there are blank pages at the end of this chapter.)

Work I Enjoy

Think of a time when you were doing work that you enjoyed. Describe your work and what you liked about it? (Note: The work you enjoyed might have been with an employer, in an educational or volunteer setting, so really think about this one!)

What is your preferred learning mode? Do you learn best and easiest by reading, listening, experimenting, pondering, discussing? Why?

Describe the balance you prefer between your work and your life. (Note: This balance is unique for each one of us.)

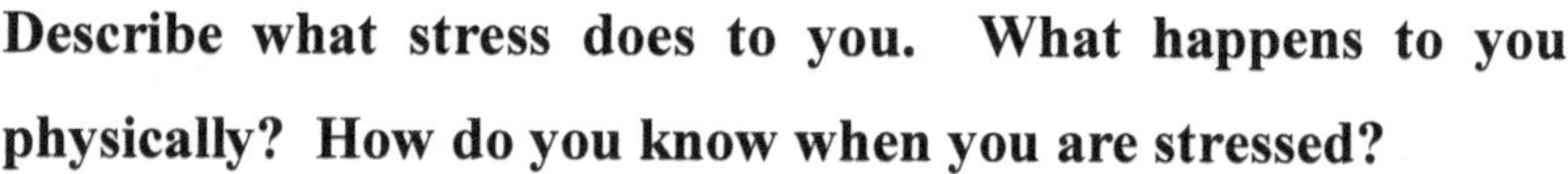

Describe what stress does to you. What happens to you physically? How do you know when you are stressed?

What are some of the things you do to neutralize stress? Do you hide-out or maybe work-out? Do you talk things over with someone? List the techniques you use to de-stress.

Describe your relationships with supervisors, business friends, network contacts, and co-workers. What do you like? What would you like more of?

Where I Am Now

What more would I like to accomplish in my career?

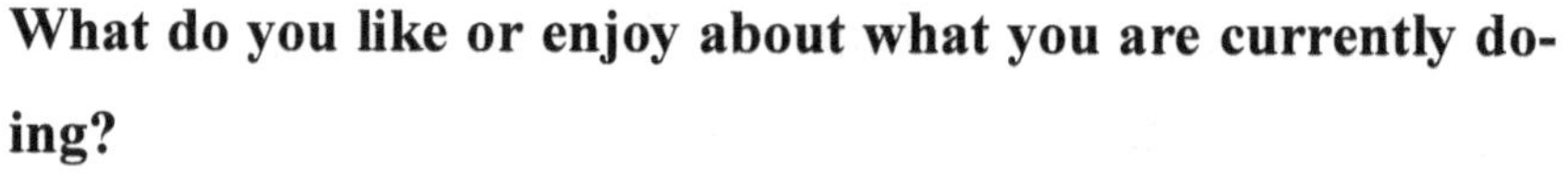

What do you like or enjoy about what you are currently doing?

Describe how changing something in your career, or growth in a new area of your life, will increase your level of satisfaction.

My Personal Life

What one thing would you change in your personal life? How would that improve your personal life?

What one thing would you NOT change? Why?

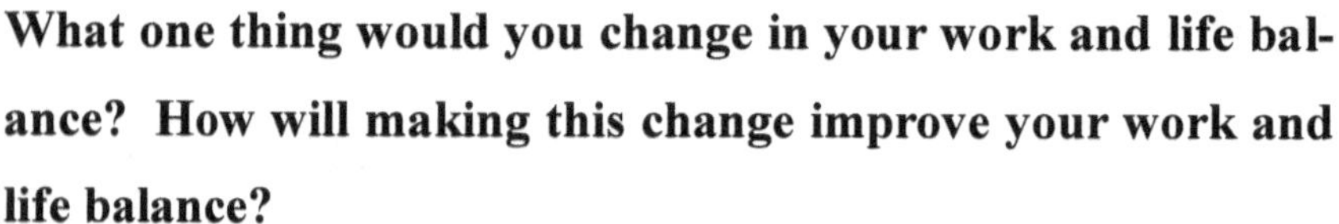

What one thing would you change in your work and life balance? How will making this change improve your work and life balance?

What characteristics does the person in your ideal relationship have? Describe what each characteristic means to you.

How will a greater level of satisfaction in your life and career affect you, your family, your relationships, and your career?

Take Action!

1. **When you are done answering the questions, take a highlighter and highlight the descriptive words that are important to you.**
2. **These are key words and we will show you how to use them.**
3. **Note: To find your descriptive words, look for words that describe an important underlying meaning for you. Words like *fair, balanced, independence, creative, accepted, limitless, and intriguing* are examples of words that may be present. If you want to include words like *successful, money, CEO, etc.*, try asking yourself the question; "*What does it mean to me to be***

***(successful, or CEO, or to have money)*?" Or, just let these words be what they are.**

4. **Transfer your highlighted words into the Descriptive Word Summary matrix on page 58 in this workbook.**

Chapter Three

Extra Worksheet Pages

Extra Worksheet Pages:

Chapter Four

Your Key Factors

My Personal Gold Standard

This chapter will provide you with a surprising amount of information about the key factors that must be present in any situation or environment in order for you to feel satisfied and enjoy yourself. A Personal Gold Standard is similar to the Gold Standard used in product development. It is the benchmark against which you can compare any potential career or life change. When you use your Personal Gold Standard in this way your choices will succeed naturally and you'll find your success rewarding. Your Personal Gold Standard is the tested and validated success program that will bring you the life and career satisfaction most people only dream of.

Using the Personal Gold Standards Process

The worksheets on the next several pages contain a process that will help you uncover the values that bring you satisfaction and enjoyment. The worksheets use Appreciate Inquiry[1] questions and are based on a format developed by Coach for Life[2]. The questions focus your attention on discovering the things you value in your business and work environment.

You can use these questions to uncover your own unique success stories and to discover your personal Gold Standards. Your Gold Standards are the underlying requirement for career satisfaction for you as an individual and knowing them will help you make the choices that will bring you contentment, fulfillment, and success. To complete this exercise, follow the next four steps.

Author's note: Your personal Gold Standards are very important to the success and enjoyment you experience in setting and achieving your personal goals. When you check a new idea, career opportunity, or service program for alignment with your Personal Gold Standards you have a very powerful tool for ensuring success and enjoyment. Make a commitment to use your

---

[2] www.coachforlife.com

Personal Gold Standards to make career choices and notice how your satisfaction expands!

Take Action!

Step 1: Answer the eight questions shown on the following pages. Take your time and really enjoy whatever memory or story comes up for you as you think about each question. You might want to record your answers on blank pages, available at the end of this chapter, so you have plenty of room to write.

Step 1a: When you are done answering the questions, take a highlighter of your choice and highlight the descriptive words that are important to you.

Reminder: To find your descriptive words look for words that describe an important underlying feeling or meaning for you. Words like fair, balanced, independence, creative, accepted, limitless, and intriguing are examples of words that may be present. If you want to include words like successful, money, CEO, etc., try asking yourself the question; "What does it mean to me to be (successful, or CEO, or to have money)?" Or just let these words be what they are and include them in the worksheet.

Gold Standards Inquiry

Find a quiet and relaxing place. Get comfortable and put aside any concerns of the day that may be on your mind. When you are ready, answer the following questions.

Remember a time when you felt "on your game" in your job, an assignment, or while training for a career. What led you to that moment? What brought you happiness and satisfaction? What is the most important thing you gained from the experience? What do you know to be absolutely true about yourself that you will take into any career?

People seek you out in business and in life to learn from you and draw from your strengths. What are your personal attributes that make you attractive and sought out by others?

Describe the attributes of other people that you seek out to learn from and to draw strength and guidance from. What is it about the people you seek out that increases your own sense of empowerment and enjoyment by virtue of associating with them?

Step 2: Transfer the descriptive words you have highlighted to the Summary sheet on page 58.

(You will already have some words on this worksheet from the Personal Reality Check exercise.)

Author's Note: Aim for 25-50 descriptive words to add to your summary sheet. If you only have a few, please feel free to go back and review the Gold Standards questions to see if you can bring forward an even deeper set of answers. As you move to step 3, remember that all your descriptive words are valuable and uniquely "you."

In the next steps, you will be able to see where they all fit in. See the next example.

Descriptive Word Summary List

Example showing a sample list of descriptive words

creative solutions	intelligent	
cost-effective	authentic people	
integrity	comfortable "in their skin" (approval-free, confi-dent, happy, low stress)	
honest	free-thinkers	
financial success (respected, freedom, good stewardship)	sharing my thoughts (generous, pass it on, completed cycle)	
creative	happy and bright	
persistence	enjoy fun	
wisdom	confident and upbeat	
courage in decision making	strength	
leadership	equal	
confidence		
knowledge		
willingness to share		
individual		

Step 3: Now go through your list of descriptive words and choose the #1, most-important descriptive word of all those listed. Repeat this process for your #2, most-important descriptive word; then for your #3, #4, and #5 most important descriptive word choices. Here is an example.

Example showing sample words from the Descriptive Word Summary with the top five highlighted in bold type font.

Creative solutions	Intelligent	
Cost-effective	authentic people	
Integrity	comfortable "in their skin"	
Honest	**free-thinkers **(5)**	
Financial success	Sharing my thoughts.	
Creative **(4)	happy and bright	
Persistence	enjoy fun	
Wisdom **(2)	**confident and up-beat **(3)**	
Courage in decision making	Strength	
leadership	Equal	
confidence	**respected **(1)**	
knowledge		
Willingness to share		
Individual		

Author's note: This can sometimes seem like a hard choice. Don't worry. Just review the words until one of them really stands out or if you get stuck, just choose one and know that it is okay.

Draw a line through that value or put asterisks next to it and record it on the Gold Standard worksheet on page 59. The example below shows the five values from the list above transferred to a Gold Standard Worksheet.

Gold Standard Worksheet

(Example: from the Gold Standards Exercise in the previous example)

In the first column, put your # 1 Descriptive Word first. It is your # 1 Gold Standard value.

Repeat this step until you have 3 or 4 Gold Standard values.

Gold Standard value	More descriptive words for this Gold Standard value
Respected	
Wisdom	
Confident and Upbeat	
Creative	
Free-thinker	

Step 3a: You now have your primary Gold Standards. Return to your list of Descriptive Words and see how many of them fit with, or compliment, your primary values. The idea is to use additional descriptive words to deeply express the meaning of each of your primary Gold Standards. You may use all of the remaining words, or just a subset. You can even make up new words that seem to make sense to you when you think about the meaning of your Gold Standards values.

Example:

Here is an example of a Gold Standards Worksheet with primary values and added descriptive words.

Gold Standard value	More descriptive words for this Gold Standard value
Respected	Integrity, Honest, Good Steward
Wisdom	Authentic, Willing to share, Knowledge, Persistence
Confident and Upbeat	Happy and bright, Fun, Confidence, Leadership
Creative	Creative Solutions, Open Minded, Intelligent

Step 4: Congratulations! You have successfully identified your top Gold Standards and increased their value by expanding on what they mean for you. These first column values will be known as your Gold Standards. When you plan actions or adopt goals and strategies, aligning them with your Gold Standards can help ensure you have both enjoyment and success. Remember that all the words recorded on your Summary List sheet are important.

Here are the worksheets for your Personal Gold Standards exercise.

1. **Go through your list of descriptive words on page 58 and choose the #1, most-important descriptive word of all those listed.**

2. **Repeat this process for your #2, most-important descriptive word; then for your #3, #4, and #5 most important descriptive word choices.**

3. **Return to your list of Descriptive Words and see how many of them fit with, or compliment, your primary values.**

4. **Use additional descriptive words to drill down on the meaning of each of your primary Gold Standards.**

5. **You may use all of the remaining words, or just a subset. You can even make up new words that seem to make sense to you when you think about the meaning of your Gold Standards values.**

Descriptive Word Summary

Gold Standard Worksheet

Take Action!

1. **In the first column, put your # 1 Descriptive Word first – it is your # 1 Personal Gold Standard. Repeat this step until you have 3 or 4 Personal Gold Standards.**

2. **In the second column, choose words from your list that you haven't used yet (or add other words you think of) to add more depth and meaning to each Personal Gold Standard in the first column.**

3. **Repeat this step until you have several descriptive words for each Personal Gold Standard.**

Gold Standard value	**More descriptive words for this Gold Standard value**

Congratulations! You have successfully identified your top Gold Standards and increased their value by expanding on what they mean for you. These first column values will be known as your Gold Standards. When you plan actions or adopt goals and strategies, aligning them with your Gold Standards can help ensure you have both enjoyment and success. Remember that all the words recorded on your Summary List sheet are important.

Now add your primary Personal Gold Standards to your Personal Project Plan on page 138.

In our next chapters, you will learn how to use your Gold Standards as a planning tool for creating a satisfying and rewarding career for yourself. You will want to keep these results of your Personal Gold Standards exercise for future reference.

Chapter Four

Extra Worksheet Pages:

Chapter Four

Extra Worksheet Pages:

Chapter Five

5

What is 'Next' for me?

In addition to your Gold Standard values, what techniques are available for picking a job, career, business, or career advancement opportunity that you'll be glad you chose? Many times, we are afraid to try something new because we might find we dislike it and then feel as though we've failed.

Remember, the *Vocational Vision* career program will lead you through the process of connecting your Gold Standard values and work preferences and show you how to create a strategy for filtering any new or existing opportunity that comes your way.

These next exercises will help you focus on and understand the priorities of your requirements for an enjoyable, rewarding, and satisfying career. You will also begin to set objectives and goals for accomplishing your career transformation.

Exercise 1: 10 Things I've wanted to do (or be) as a Career

In this exercise, please think about the career or business ideas you have had during your life. You can go as far back as you wish – just try to write down ten (10) of them. You are free to write down more or less than ten if you want to.

When you are done, go back and write down what it was about each of those careers or businesses that was important to you. For example: What interested you about the assignment, career or business? What was fun or enjoyable? What type of relationships interested you? How did the level of responsibility for that assignment, career or business satisfy you? In the second column, try to capture a small paragraph describing the "juice" of interest that each assignment, career or business opportunity meant to you.

Career	**What I Liked About the Career**

Exercise 2: Career Preferences

This exercise will help you set the scope for your career preferences. These are the things you enjoy doing. Try to get underneath the title or surface description of each answer. For each question, also ask yourself *WHY do I like this? Or, WHAT do I like about this?*

What do you like to do most? What is it that you find most enjoyable?

What activity (activities) are the most fun for you? Why is that?

When I am doing ________ I feel alive, satisfied, and fully empowered! Describe what being fully empowered means to you.

What is something you would do even if you didn't get paid for it? What do you volunteer for? Do you have a hobby? If you feel stuck on this question, describe the different kind of reward (pay, recognition, etc.) that you like.

Describe a project you worked on. What were the contributions you made? How did your contribution help make the project successful?

Describe a time when you felt that you were empowered and effective in your organization, team or group. What were the key characteristics you embodied that made your actions so powerful and effective?

Describe a time when you felt very excited and happy doing something (either alone or with a group). What made it so fulfilling for you?

Pretend you "fast-forward" five years into the future. What is your lifestyle? What work are you doing? What are your relationships with family and friends like? Is there someone special in your life? If so describe him/her. Are you solo? If so, are you content or seeking a relationship?

Exercise 3: Where I Want to Be in the Future?

Where do I want to be in my career?

One year from now?

Two years from now?

Five years from now?

Exercise 4: Personal Satisfaction

Go to Figure 1 below and follow the instructions to discover your current personal satisfaction level.

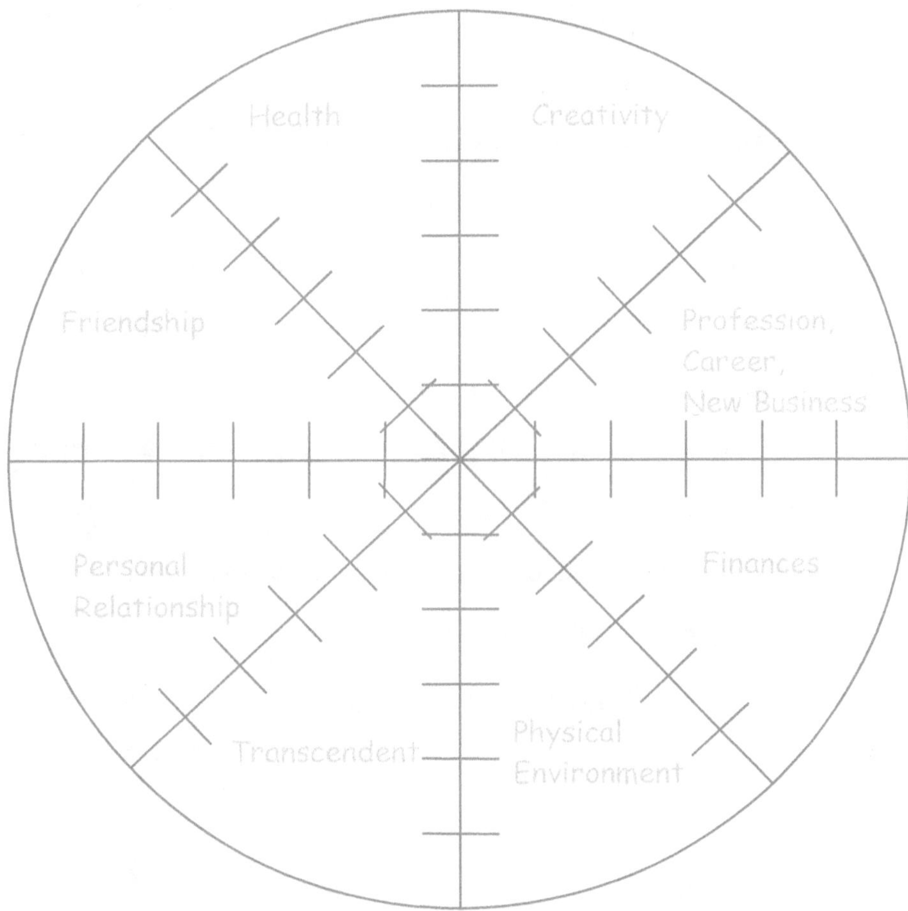

Health – Your body, health, wellness, physical safety

Friendship – Your relationships with Neighbors, Work Colleagues, Business Partners

Personal Relationship – Your primary relationships, Spouse, Significant Other, Family, Siblings

Transcendent – Your connection with an all-powerful universal force or being or where you go to seek answers to the "big questions" of life

Physical Environment – Your satisfaction with your home, office, car or other places where you spend time

Finances – Your relationship with giving and receiving money, resources, and abundance

Profession, Career, New Business – Your satisfaction with your work, giving and expressing your gifts, talents and experience

Creativity – Your creative expression in art, music, word, fashion, culinary art, crafts, construction, etc.

Take Action!

Rate your satisfaction now by placing an X on the segment. 0 [origin] = "not at all satisfied"; 10 [outer edge] = "100%satisfied")

Where would you like to be on each? Circle the value on the wheel where you would like to be right now for each spoke.

What one personal satisfaction segment do I want to change most right now? Describe on the following lines what that segment would be like for you at the rating you desire.

____

____

____

____

____

____

____

Now highlight the key words from these four exercises. Prioritize your key words and write the top 8-12 in the spaces below.

Key Words for My Career and Life Change Preferences

When you are done:

1. **Compare to Personal Gold Standards from page 59. Can you now see some of those values "at work" in the careers and businesses that have interested you over the years? Notice the values that are showing up most often.**

2. **Look for patterns. Look for the common threads that exist in the careers and business opportunities you have in your list. Be assured that there are common values, responsibilities, and service opportunities that are an integral part of who you are.**

3. **Prioritize your key words from page 74 above. You now have a list of criteria based upon things that you have wanted to do or be (career-wise) and the essence of what these careers or business opportunities mean to you. In the space below, list your key criteria in descending order of important and/or meaning to you**

My Prioritized List of Criteria for a Satisfying Career

Enter the top 5 or 6 criteria into your Personal Project Plan on page 139 in the "My Career and life Requirements" section.

Goals and Targets for a Satisfying Career or Life

Thinking about your criteria above, describe 1-3 outcomes (goals, objectives, targets) that you would enjoy focusing on and that would allow you to enjoy upgrading something in your life.

____

____

____

____

____

Highlight the key words and transfer these to the Goals and Objectives Summary sheet below.

We will use these key words to create the objective statement for your Personal Project Plan.

Objectives and Goals Summary

____

____

____

____

____

Now choose the top three (3) goals or objectives that you want to start working on.

SMART Objectives

The next exercise will help you write objectives statements that are SMART.

The most effective template for creating objectives that are focused and achievable is to use the acronym S.M.A.R.T. Here is the acronym explained:

Specific: The objective is described sufficiently that it is possible to determine the degree to which it has been accomplished or completed.

Measurable: The objective can be objectively measured.

Ambitious: The objective is something that is a stretch for you and is something that you would truly like to accomplish.

Results oriented: The objective has a clear result and the result has an overall impact on what you want to accomplish.

Time bound: The objective has a definite time frame in which it will be accomplished.

This may take a little bit of practice before you feel comfortable with the process. Here are some examples of SMART objectives that you may find helpful.

SMART Objectives Examples

Keyword(s) from Summary Sheet	Objective	SMART
Home office based	Establish a home office with telephone, fax, printer, computer, and Internet access by end 1st Qtr. 20xx*	Y
Travel to clients	Create customer relationships with a local client base of 8-10 small business people by 12/31/20xx*	Y
$75K yearly or more	In 20xx, generate a minimum of $75k yearly income from all sources. (This is approximately $6300 in billable services or salary each month.)	Y

"Green" company	Research all local companies and find out which ones have "green" environmental policies. Apply to 3 "green" companies by end-June 20xx*	Y
Leverage what I already know	Rework my resume content to reflect the current status of my knowledge and experience. Research what is currently popular in resume formats and choose one that I like. Have an updated, focused, and modern resume by 1/31/20xx*	Y
Opportunity for creativity	Prepare a list of questions to use during interviews that will help me uncover the potential for creativity in new job or career opportunities. Have the list available by end of January, 20xx*	Y

* **Author's note:**

Please use current year dates for your objectives.

Take Action!

Transfer your SMART objectives to your Personal Project Plan on page 139 under My Goal and Objective Statements.

Chapter Five

Extra Worksheet Pages:

Chapter Five

Extra Worksheet Pages:

Chapter Six

Charting Progress on your (P3)

Your P3 is your "Personal Project Plan" (PPP or P3).

Charting your progress is a great way to keep your momentum going. The key is to choose milestones and proof points that are meaningful to you and that create a stairway to your success. Just as in the construction of a staircase for your home or place of business, the foundation for your stairway must be solid. The P3 you are constructing as part of this workbook provides you with a firm platform. Your milestones and tasks in-between milestones will give you the risers and treads for your staircase. Make a commitment to yourself to choose them wisely!

The Basics of Good Milestones

What is a good milestone? Here are several characteristics that typify a well-defined milestone.

- **Clear**
  A good milestone is specific and understandable

- **Meaningful**
  A good milestone represents an accomplishment toward your goal

- **Measure Progress**
  A good milestone provides useful information about whether or not you are on track to achieve your ultimate goal

- **Achievable**
  A good milestone is one that you feel confident you can achieve by its due date and are willing to commit to

- **Right-sized**
  A good milestone is big enough to give you a feeling of satisfaction when you accomplishment it but not so big that it seems a dangerous "long-shot"

Create a kickoff phase for your career project.

Now, let's begin to build the milestones and proof points for your Personal Project Plan. Here are some questions to help you start.

What tools are you going to use to support your project? (e.g.: notebook, Excel spreadsheet, calendar, etc.)

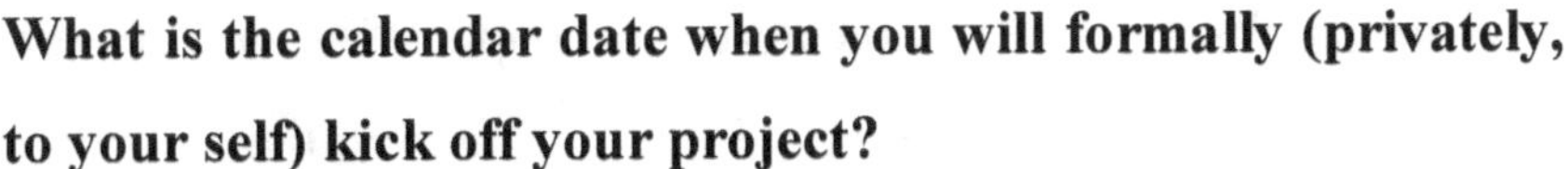

What is the calendar date when you will formally (privately, to your self) kick off your project?

What is your aiming point? How will you know that you're done? (e.g. employed in new career, promotion, business or franchise up and running, a book published, degree completed, etc.)

What calendar date would you like to choose as your target completion date for your career transition?

Now, go back to your objectives in chapter five and review the dates for your objectives. Begin by subtracting the start date from the end date to get the number of weeks of duration for your project plan. If you have a partial week, always round up to the next week. Divide the number of weeks by four to calculate the major review date interval. Create dates for each of the major reviews by adding the interval to start date and each resulting major review date. When you finish you will have a start date, three major reviews, and an end date.

At each major review you will be evaluating the progress of your plan and determining if any re-planning is required.

Example:

Milestone	**Start Date**	**End Date**	**Expected Duration**

Design Your Milestones

Milestones are checkpoints at the end of the collection of tasks. Look at each major review and answer the following questions.

1. By my first review date what part or parts of my P3 do I need to have completed to feel I am making progress?

2. What part or parts of my P3 will take the longest?

Break down each longer duration task into four smaller steps. Each step will be a milestone. [If the task is more complex, you can subdivide further into smaller milestones.]

Choose a date for your milestones so that you can check them at your next review date and evaluate their percentage of completion. Keep doing this until you have milestone dates for each task.

Take Action!

Add all your milestones and review dates to your P3 on page 140.

Chapter Seven

Strategy for Success

Knowing what you want and successfully accomplishing it requires a strategy. Not just any strategy will do. You will succeed most easily and quickly if you build your strategy in a way that is customized to your personal strengths and preferences. This chapter will help you build a personalized and customized strategic plan for accomplishing your career transition goals and objectives.

Answer the following questions to begin uncovering the techniques you've used in previous successful projects. We will show you how to use the underlying architecture of these techniques in your Personal Project Plan.

Strategies for Accomplishment

Describe a successful project or assignment, either in your life or business career, and what and how you contributed to its success.

What strategies and ways of approaching getting something done have worked for you in the past? How did your actions and activities contribute to your achievements?

What one strategy or approach for getting things done haven't you tried that you think might work?

Take Action!

Highlight the key words and transfer these to the Success Strategies Summary worksheet on page 95.

The Foundation for Success

Every career is built on creating and establishing a foundation that defines who you are and how others experience you. The skills and interests already developed in your career are part of this foundation.

Studies also show that successful careers have the following six (6) skills at their foundation: *persistence, communication, business savvy, skill, reliability, and attitude*.

For your successful career or life transition, we encourage you to integrate growth in these six (6) basic and foundational skill areas. They don't need to be worked on as a group, so feel free to score yourself on your skill level today and then choose a competency that you feel will give you the most return on an investment of your time and talent.

On the next few pages, these six key skills are defined. You will have an opportunity to create power strategies for yourself to ensure that these keys to being successful are included in your Personal Project Plan.

The Basic Competencies (Skills)

What are the Basic Competencies for a successful career? Are there really a set of career skills and attitudes that make a difference between success, happiness and promotion and being stuck in a dead-end job or living a dull life?

We believe there is a basic set of career skills (i.e. areas of competence) possessed by those people who consistently find success in their careers. Here's the list:

1. **Persistence (ensure what is started is finished)**
2. **Communication (working well with teams, external and internal customers, in both speaking and writing)**
3. **Business Savvy (understanding the business engaged in and where his/her career fits into the bigger picture for the company or business)**
4. **Skill (commitment to gaining and maintaining skill in a career area)**
5. **Reliability (can be counted on to support the business, customers, and the team when needed)**
6. **Attitude (professional attitude appropriate for career, personal details limited to what is appropriate for the business culture)**

Take Action!

Competency	My Current Level Scale of 1-10	My Next Target Level Scale of 1-10	My abilities at target level
Persistence			
Communication			
Business Savvy			
Skill			
Reliability			
Attitude			

What one of the Basic Competencies for a successful career would you like to expand on in the coming year?

What benefits might this bring to your group, organization, or company?

Take Action!

Choose one of these common or "core" competencies for career success and add it to your Goals and Objectives Summary worksheet on page 77.

Write a SMART objective for it and add it to your Personal Project Plan on page 139.

Powerful Personal Success Strategies

Success Strategies Key Words Summary Sheet

From exercises on page 90

Go back through your Success Strategies Key Words above and choose the #1 key word that will help you the most in rapidly and easily achieving your goals and objectives. Repeat this process to find the 2nd, 3rd, 4th and 5th keywords that will help you build a successful strategy.

Create your success strategy Power Statements by creating a strong sentence using your top three or four keywords using the template below.

Power Strategy #1:

I WILL (or I WILL USE MY ABILITY)

____ to help me achieve my goals and objectives.

Power Strategy #2:

I WILL (or I WILL USE MY ABILITY)

____ to help me achieve my goals and objectives.

Power Strategy #3:

I WILL (or I WILL USE MY ABILITY)

____ to help me achieve my goals and objectives.

Power Strategy #4:

I WILL (or I WILL USE MY ABILITY)

____ to help me achieve my goals and objectives.

Take Action!

Transfer these to your Personal Project Plan on page 139 under My Success Strategies.

For Example:

Let's assume that our top four Success Strategy key words are:

Persistence; creative problem solving; ask a trusted advisor for help; give myself a subconscious suggestion to find an answer

Our Power Strategy #1 might be:

I WILL use Persistence to help me achieve my goals and objectives.

Power Strategy # 2 might be:

I WILL use my ability for creative problem solving to help me achieve my goals and objectives.

Power Strategy #3 might be:

I WILL ask a Trusted Advisor to help me achieve my goals and objectives.

Power Strategy #4 might be:

I WILL use Subconscious Suggestions to help me achieve my goals and objectives.

Chapter Seven

Extra Worksheet Pages:

Chapter Eight

Your Personal Plan of Action

Using a Personal Project Plan

Just like a hardware or software development Project Plan, a Personal Project Plan (P3) will keep you focused on what needs to be done next. Your P3 will also help you identify as early as possible any roadblocks or risks to your success. By addressing any of these roadblocks or problems early, you can avoid costly mistakes – mistakes that could seriously impact completing your personal growth project.

The P3 doesn't have to be fancy or complicated. It just needs to be an easy and convenient way for you to collect your goals, milestones, accomplishments, changes, and risks. Include a section for objectives and leave space under each objective for some tasks and sub-tasks. Include a section for a timeline and decide how you want to track milestones and mini-milestones.

Take a few moments right now and look over the template in Chapter 12. This Personal Project Plan is included for your convenience in the *Vocational Vision: Defining Your Talent for a Successful Career* book, and you've been building it as you worked through the previous chapters. However, you can use whatever method works best for you. It is very important for you to create a tool that you want to use. Pick a format that you like; create your Personal Project Plan and begin to use and maintain it for the duration of your project!

Implementing Your Personal Project Plan (P3)

No matter how good and capable you are (and you are very capable), there will be moments in the implementation of your Personal Project Plan that will challenge you. For example, you may find that you need to accomplish some part of your P3 in a compressed time frame. What if you've just received a poor review or you've been surprised to learn that your favorite personal relationship may be ending? In cases like these, rapid change management may become very important to you!

At other points in your P3 you may find your goals or objectives are in need of some fine tuning or that your implementation is encountering roadblocks. In this instance, you might want to make a mid-course correction to your goals, objectives, time allocation, etc. in order to accomplish your plan in a way that you find personally satisfying.

In this next section, we will show you how to create work-arounds for rapid results and how to make mid-course corrections. We will provide you with the ideas to successfully chart your progress and create checkpoints to help ensure you successfully manage and achieve your goals.

First, we will explore with you the drivers that will make your Personal Project Plan a failsafe approach to making successful changes in your life and career. We will also help you prepare for implementing a mid-life kicker if you begin to get bored or feel overwhelmed.

Read on for the keys to successfully implementing your Personal Project Plan!

Dealing with Roadblocks and Resistance

How can you help ensure that you reach your target goals and objectives and make the needed changes in your life and career? Here are five tips to give yourself a boost if you feel yourself losing momentum.

Ensure your success by doing the exercises in this chapter.

1. **Self confidence** – Take some time and review your "I AM" statements on page 137 and your Success Strategies Summary on page 95.

   You have so much knowledge and wisdom and it has great value. You know you can do it!

2. **Time Management** – Check the milestones in your Personal Project Plan on page 140. Are there some that

need reworking? Have you set one or more milestones too aggressively? Are there any milestones that aren't challenging enough?

This is your Personal Project Plan, and you are encouraged to set your goals, objectives and milestones so that they stretch you but don't discourage you.

3. **Social Competence** – Communicating effectively and naturally will make it easier for you to accomplish you plan.

   If you need to work on your ability to communicate, do the exercise on Your Personal Communication Strategy. (See page 109).

4. **Achievement Motivation** – Review your Personal Gold Standard values on page **138**. Are you looking for these in the every day events and relationships you enjoy? Are there some areas of your life where you could make an exercise of looking for these Gold Standard values?

   When you do this type of exercise regularly, you will find greater enjoyment and satisfaction in everything.

   Remember:

Your Gold Standard Values = The Juice of Your Life

5. Intellectual Flexibility (Thinking Outside of the Box) – If you feel stuck or feel you are losing momentum do the next exercises to give yourself a boost.

Create a Mid-life Kicker

What if I get "stuck"? Why can't I get off of dead center?

Okay, it's true. Sometimes, even though we do everything according to our plan, we just get stuck. If you start to feel that you are not reaching your goals fast enough, if your close friends and family would just prefer you go back to the old way of being and making a living, or if the world at large just doesn't seem to be giving you the success you're working towards, then you need a shot of energy to get your project back on track.

What happens if I…

- **Feel resistance from family, friends, and colleagues**
- **Get bored**
- **Lose steam**
- **Need to refocus**

Here are some questions to help you move forward if you find yourself losing enthusiasm for completing your Personal Project Plan.

What does it feel like when I'm stuck? What things do I do? What self-talk or thoughts do I have?

What are the two biggest roadblocks that are getting in the way of accomplishing my goals? What roadblocks have gotten in my way before?

What makes me want to procrastinate?

What always makes me feel energetic and enthusiastic about a goal, task or project?

Chapter Eight

What is the best thing about starting a new project, task or objective?

What is the best thing about finishing a new project, task, or objective?

Take Action!

Highlight the key words from these six questions and use them to re-create some success strategies for yourself.

Create your "My Career" statement

Use the following template and your top three Gold Standard values to help define your "My Career…" statement. When you are finished, transfer your 'My Career; statement to your Personal Project Plan on page 137.

Example:
My career will satisfy my Gold Standard attributes of ***: Having fun, Beng curious minded, and Being accepted as part of a team.***

Your Turn!

My Career will satisfy my Gold Standard attributes of:

____

____

____

____

To accomplish integrating your Gold standard attributes into all your career choices, complete your "I will…" statement:

Example:

1. ***Having Fun:*** *I will seek colleagues and business cultures where there is a balance between work and play.*
2. ***Curious Minded:*** *I will seek companies and teams that give me opportunities to learn new, cutting edge technology.*
3. ***Being Accepted by Team****: I will seek teams where my contribution is eagerly received and where I can learn from others.*

Your Turn!

1. **#1:** ***I will seek*** ________________________________
   ____.
2. **#2:** ***I will seek*** ________________________________
   ____.
3. **#3:** ***I will seek****:*________________________________
   ____.

Transfer your "I Will" statements to your Personal Project Plan on page 138.

Extra Worksheet Pages

Chapter Nine

Navigating Your Project Plan

Your Personal Communication Strategy

Communicate even with those who do not easily understand you

If you are a fan of the Harry Potter books and movies, you probably recognize the term "Muggles" as a metaphor for people who do not understand or appreciate those who are intellectually, creatively, (or magically) different from themselves.

Living and interacting with people who do not understand the way you think can be a source of stress. Often others do not see the world in the same way that your technical, practical, logical, or creative mind sees it. This does not imply that other views are invalid. However it does begin to explain the value of feeling confident that one can communicate effectively with others regardless of their mindset.

Build Your Communication Skills

To begin to build your own skills in interactions with people who have previously caused stress or difficulty for you, try the following exercise.

Answer these Awareness questions about Communications Agility:

If I fast-forward in time one year from now, how would I like my ability to interact with people around me to be different?

Choose a recent or memorable example of a communication with supervisors, managers, co-workers or customers or clients and envision it changed.

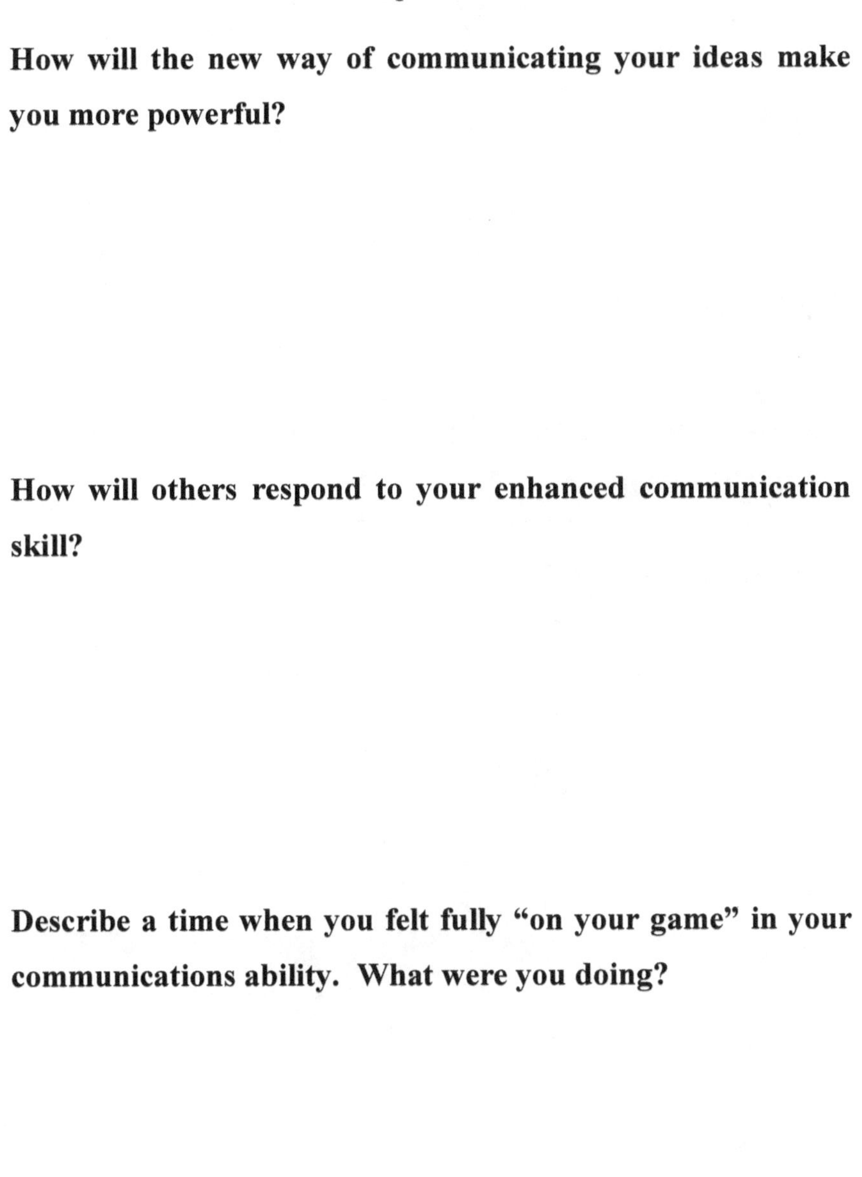

How will the new way of communicating your ideas make you more powerful?

How will others respond to your enhanced communication skill?

Describe a time when you felt fully "on your game" in your communications ability. What were you doing?

What is your inner awareness of your own empowerment?

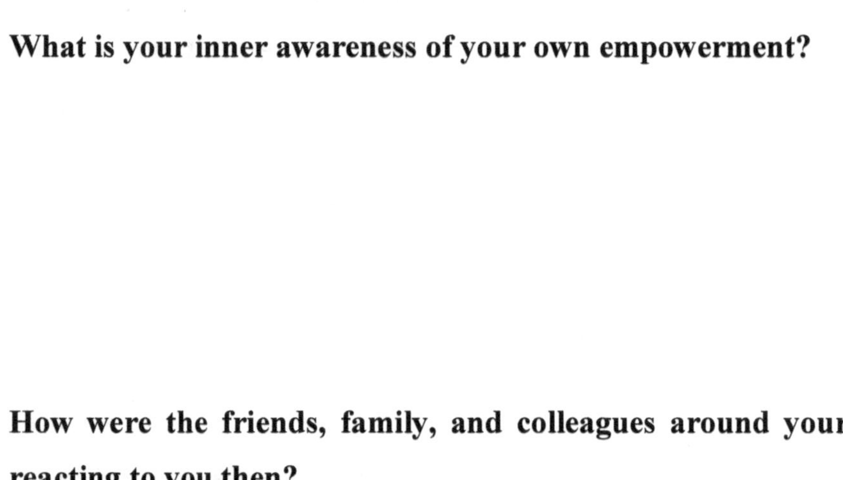

How were the friends, family, and colleagues around your reacting to you then?

Building an Enhanced Communication Plan

Take Action!

For a drill-down on enhancing your communications with people in general, managers, colleagues, clients, and customers, complete your questions using the following three steps.

1. **Highlight or underline the words in your answers in the above exercise that mean the most to you.**
2. **Put the underlined words below and rank them top to bottom for their importance to you.**
3. **Use the top five words to create an objective (or objectives) for yourself. Begin the objective with these words, "My communication with people of all backgrounds…"**

Here is an example (with key words underlined)

Pick a recent or memorable example of a communication with colleagues, managers, supervisors, or customers or clients and envision it changed.

Recently I was in a project status meeting where there was a problem being discussed. Someone asked me a question, and I didn't like the tone of voice they used. I reacted defensively and spoke sharply to them because I felt attacked. Later on, I began to think that perhaps the question was more relevant that I originally thought and that I may have over-reacted.

I would like to see this event changed so that I am able to look more at the question being asked and less at what I perceive to be the motivation of the person asking.

I would like people to listen to what I have to share and I also would like others to understand that I have listened sincerely to them.

How will the new way of communicating your ideas make you more powerful?

I will feel empowered in a balanced and respectful way but I won't be overbearing. I also won't need to have anyone agree with me. I'll be independent of their opinion and confident without defensives about my own opinion.

How will others respond to your enhanced communication skill?

Other people respond to this enhanced communication ability by opening up and feeling able to receive my ideas easily and respectfully.

Describe a time when you felt fully "on your game" in your communications ability. What were you doing?

I was speaking with a client and answering their questions about their software program.

What is your inner awareness of your own empowerment?

When I listen to the customer/client and answer their questions honestly and as completely as I can, they receive the information easily and treat me respectfully.

How were your friends, family, and colleagues reacting to you?

My colleagues and the client are listening to me, taking notes on what I have to share, and thanking me for the information.

My Exercise Key Words

empowered in a balanced and respectful way

independent of others' opinions

confident without defensiveness

sincere

able to receive and share ideas with ease

My Objective Statement:

My business communications with people will be balanced and respectful; independent of others' opinions; confident and non-defensive; sincere. I am able to receive and share ideas with ease.

Now, it is your turn to do this exercise.

Pick a recent or memorable example of a communication with colleagues, managers, supervisors, or customers or clients and envision it changed.

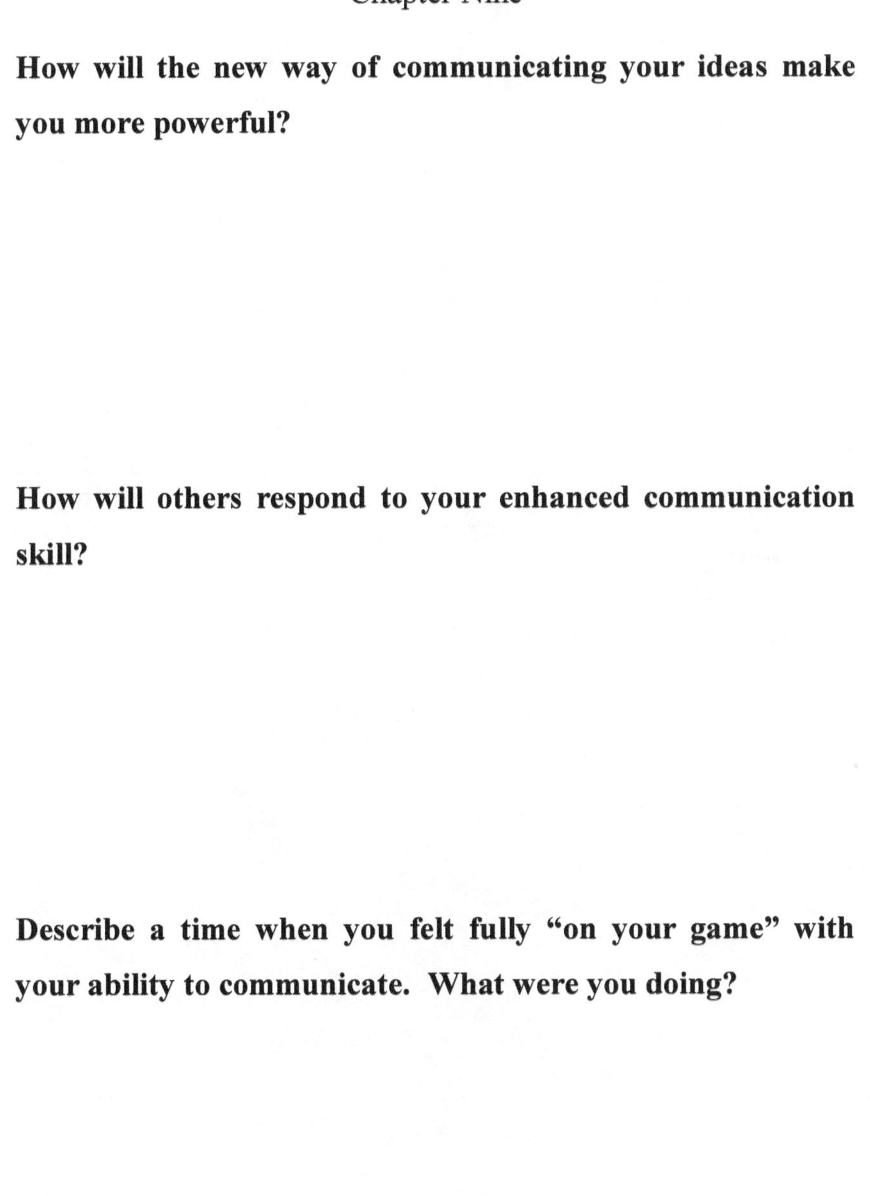

How will the new way of communicating your ideas make you more powerful?

How will others respond to your enhanced communication skill?

Describe a time when you felt fully "on your game" with your ability to communicate. What were you doing?

What is your inner awareness of your own empowerment?

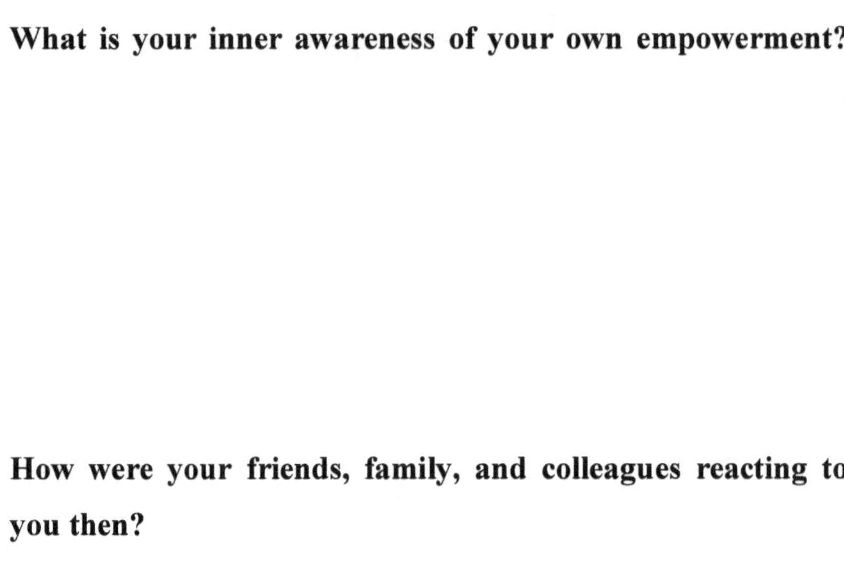

How were your friends, family, and colleagues reacting to you then?

My Choice

The choice is truly yours to make. You can continue to communicate as you always have or you can begin today to make a few, significant changes that will benefit your life and career for many years. An "I Choose" statement is a declaration of your aiming point for yourself.

Use one of more the following templates to help define your "I Choose…" Statement:

I choose to enhance my ability to communicate so that I will be more …. <add your top three underlined words>

For example: I choose to improve my ability to communicate so that I will be more empowered in a balanced and respectful way. I will be more independent of others' opinions and confident without being defensive.

Other "I Choose…" Statement(s):

I choose to enhance my ability to communicate so that I will be more …. <add your top three underlined words>

By improving my ability to communicate I will have more… <add your top three underlined words>

As my ability to communicate increases, people around me will see me as … <add your top three underlined words>

Take Action!

Create your own "I Choose" statement using the space below and add it to page 138. You may also find it helpful to create a SMART objective for communicating with others. Be sure to add it to your Personal Project Plan in the Objectives section (page 139).

I CHOOSE______________________________________

Chapter Nine

Extra Worksheet Pages:

Chapter Nine

Extra Worksheet Pages:

Chapter Ten

10

Dig Out the Bugs

Keep Your Momentum and Overcome Resistance

Be on the lookout for Resistance, Risks and Roadblocks that try to get in your way. Resistance is completely normal. It isn't fun or enjoyable but it actually serves a purpose. Resistance allows you to examine where you are and either reaffirm your goals or make mid-project corrections. When resistance to your project plan objectives and goals appears, you have options. You can recommit yourself to your project plan and find a work-around, or modification, or fix for your resistance. Avoid the temptation to abandon your plan and terminate your project.

When resistance happens in a business project these same options are present. Usually at work we use every resource possible to overcome the resistance that threatens our project(s). In our personal life and career projects we can also use every resource possible to triumph over the threat to our success.

Often it is difficult to recognize resistance in our own personal projects. Here are some common guises that illustrate the presence of resistance.

1. **I'm too tired to do this.**
2. **My family isn't helping me through this.**
3. **This should be easier. I shouldn't have to struggle.**
4. **I'm too old (or set in my ways.)**
5. **It's not really worth it.**

1. [Add your own resistance "bugs" here after the next exercise]
2. [Add your own resistance "bugs" here after the next exercise]
3. [Add your own resistance "bugs" here after the next exercise]
4. [Add your own resistance "bugs" here after the next exercise]

How does resistance show up for you?

In what common ways does resistance show up in your projects? Take a few moments and answer these questions:

In your last assignment or work project what felt risky or difficult? What external or internal events, people, or situations threatened your project plan schedule?

Think about a New Year's resolution you made in the past and fast-forward about two months. Did you have any resistance to completing your resolution? Write down any resistance you felt and what you did to overcome it.

Take Action!

Raise your awareness of when and how resistance appears in your daily life. Give yourself permission to have resistance and to be able to manage it. Here is an exercise to help you begin to notice the presence of resistance.

Use the Eureka Method.

For one week, every time you recognize resistance to improving your self confidence – say to yourself – "Eureka! I found one"

Write your resistance "bugs" in the following blank space. After one week, pick your top 3-5 resistance bugs and add them to the list on page 124.

Fixing your Resistance "Bugs"

Just like in the movie, Stargate Troopers, a "bug" is: something (a belief, behavior, or technique) that we've used successfully in the past but that no longer serves our needs (and can create quite a bit of mischief in our lives.)

"Bugs" can be:

Thoughts, feelings, beliefs, and behaviors that used to work for us but now work to prevent us from growing and changing.

A "Bug" needs:

A bug needs something else to work on to help us be successful in our new, desired, career or line of work. This next exercise will help you to reformat your resistance bugs into useful work for accomplishing your current objectives and goals.

Take Action!

Go back to your list of Resistance Bugs (page 124) and transfer the ones that "bug" you the most to your Personal Project Plan in the Bug Busters section on page 140. Follow each bug with an idea or two about how to overcome the resistance (aka Resistance Busters.)

Here are some sample answers to illustrate.

Resistance: ***It isn't happening fast enough.***

Resistance Buster: Check your timeline expectations. Are they reasonable? Adjust if they are overly optimistic or pessimistic. See if you are using unrealistic expectations as an excuse to lose focus on your objective.

Resistance: ***I start to worry about money. When I make changes, the flow of money also changes. Sometime I worry that it will be harder to make enough money to live on, etc.***

Resistance Buster: Keep the momentum going on my project plan. Carve out some time to make myself available for fill-in work to ease worries over money. Be open to receiving compensation in forms different from my old line of work.

Resistance: ***My friends and family don't really want me to change. They are comfortable with me in my old work situation. It's predictable. They want me to be happy with where I was.***

Resistance Buster: Recognize that the resistance of friends and family is their resistance, not mine. They care for me but would prefer that I not change. Begin to cultivate new (additional) friends, business colleagues and groups that are willing and able to see me in my new career.

Chapter Ten

Extra Worksheet Pages:

Chapter Eleven

11

Commitment, Acceptance, Integration

Commitment

As you progress through your Personal Project Plan you may find yourself losing interest, having trouble completing some of the exercises, or just beginning to wonder if you really want to do this work. This is a common part of the process so don't feel discouraged. If you find yourself losing steam on your journey to realize your personal project plan, here are some ideas you can use to revitalize your commitment and have the career that satisfies and fulfills you.

Commit to improving your self confidence

Be creative and resourceful! Use books, coaching, friends, mentors and spiritual growth techniques to help you improve your self confidence. As your self confidence improves, your ability to successfully follow your Personal Project Plan improves as well. Look for ways to support your confidence in achieving the career you desire. Use any of the suggestions below to help yourself. Your effort will have a huge payback.

Review and define your goals and objectives

If you feel your commitment slipping or feel that you're losing momentum try redefining your goals and objectives. Take a look at the aiming points you have set for yourself and see if they are things you still truly want to do.

Rebuild momentum with an awareness exercise

Redo the Step 1 exercise from Chapter 4 on page 49. If needed, use your new results to fine tune your goals and objectives.

Read your "I Choose" statements daily

Re-read your "I Choose" statements every day to help you remember what you have chosen to do and why it is important to you.

Look for and review resistance bugs

Resistance to change is a very normal part of this process. If you begin to feel internal resistance to completing exercise in the workbook, or performing self-reviews, or even wondering if it is worthwhile to complete these exercises, you are experiencing resistance. Go back to Chapter 10 and review the exercises on identifying resistance and providing resistance busters. See if there are some things that you can do to overcome the resistance you are feeling. Look for old habits hiding out as resistance bugs. If they need a new job, give them one!

Are your goals and objectives SMART?

Another stumbling block to commitment can occur if your goals and objectives are not following the SMART formula.

Maybe your goals and objectives are SMART, but some of the "SMART" characteristics are not working for you. Change them until they feel like a perfect fit for what you want to accomplish.

Make sure you are comfortable with each of the points in your SMART characteristics. If not, change them. This will help you remain committed to reaching the goals and objectives in your P3.

Review your Awareness exercise

If you really feel like you are struggling with staying committed to your personal Project plan, go back and redo the awareness exercise in the beginning of this book. This will help you remember what is important to you in making this career change and why these choices are so important to you.

Retune if Needed

Remind yourself of the importance of what you are accomplishing and retune if needed. Recognize that you may need to redo some of your awareness exercises, some of your goals, and/or some of your "I Choose" and "I Am" statements in order to create the project plan that will work for you and that will help you accomplish your career goals.

Acceptance and Integration

What does struggle mean to you? How would you define its opposite, "ease?" For some, struggle means forcing themselves to get up, go to work, and trudge through the workdays, endlessly waiting for the weekend to come. When the weekend comes, the relief may feel short lived because the beginning of the next work week hangs ominously like a dark cloud. If you have ever felt depressed on Sunday because Monday was coming, you are very likely not doing work you enjoy. So use these exercises and your P3 to make your work life something that fulfills you. You will find that your weekends, vacations, and days off are much more enjoyable without that dark cloud of unsatisfying work looming ahead of you. You have an excellent opportunity to choose a path that works FOR you, not against you.

As you work your P3, your Personal Project Plan, it becomes easier and more natural. This is similar to practicing a sport, musical instrument, or dance step. The more time you focus on your plan, the more it becomes your norm. But beware. Your P3 will take you to whatever you create. If you want your norm to be fulfilling and satisfying you must honestly create a Personal Project Plan that pulls you toward the proper endpoint for you. The goals and objectives need to be yours, not what someone else thinks will satisfy you but what you now know (from these exercises) will satisfy you.

Understand that the shift from struggle to ease occurs most rapidly when you create and commit to a plan that is truly in alignment with what you like and what you want. This does not mean that self-discipline, dedication, and authentic responsibility are no longer required. What it does mean is the energy you put into self-discipline, dedication to your work, and acting responsibly will no longer drain you. You will find a vast reservoir of energy for work, family, friendships, and play that naturally restores itself.

The old self doubt is in the past and the "new, self confident you" feels (and is) normal.

As you gain confidence in the value of your P3, you will discover that you gain confidence in yourself. The impact of your growth and success is influenced greatly by the extent to which you have aligned your P3 objectives with the things you authentically enjoy and find pleasure in doing. Make reaching this point truly transformative for yourself in a positive and financially satisfying way.

You have been given the gift of this life. I challenge you and encourage you to live it as a satisfied, happy, fulfilled person.

Vocational Vision: Defining Your Talent for a Successful Career is my gift to you to achieve all that satisfies and supports you in achieving all that you are destined to do.

Chapter Eleven

Extra Worksheet Pages:

Your Personal Project Plan Templates

Use this template to create your Personal Project Plan. Copy your answers to the exercises in the *Vocational Vision: Defining Your Talent for a Successful Career* book to the sections in this template as indicated in each exercise.

My Personal Project Plan

My I AM Statements

____

____

____

____

My Career Statement(s)

____

____

My I WILL Statements

My I CHOOSE Communication Statement

My Gold Standard Values

My Career and Life Requirements

My Goal and Objective Statements

My Success Strategies

Bug Busters for Resistance, Risks, and Roadblocks

Resistance, Roadblock or Risk (i.e. the Bug)	My Resistance Busting Strategy

Milestones

Milestone	Expected Date	Actual Date	Best Practices

Chapter Twelve

Extra Worksheet Pages:

Chapter Twelve

Extra Worksheet Pages:

www.ingramcontent.com/pod-product-compliance
Lightning Source LLC
Chambersburg PA
CBHW030801180526
45163CB00003B/1116
* 9 7 8 0 5 5 7 2 3 1 5 2 2 *